The Constitution

John Hamilton

ABDO
Publishing Company

visit us at
www.abdopub.com

Published by ABDO Publishing Company, 4940 Viking Drive, Edina, Minnesota 55435.
Copyright © 2005 by Abdo Consulting Group, Inc. International copyrights reserved in all
countries. No part of this book may be reproduced in any form without written permission from
the publisher. The Checkerboard Library™ is a trademark and logo of ABDO Publishing
Company.

Printed in the United States.

Cover Photos: Corbis
Interior Photos: Corbis pp. 1, 5, 9, 10, 15, 16, 18, 19, 22, 23, 27; Getty Images p. 29;
    Library of Congress pp. 12, 20; North Wind pp. 6, 7, 11, 31

Series Coordinator: Kristin Van Cleaf
Editors: Tamara L. Britton, Jennifer R. Krueger, Kristin Van Cleaf
Art Direction & Maps: Neil Klinepier

Library of Congress Cataloging-in-Publication Data

Hamilton, John, 1959-
    The Constitution / John Hamilton.
       p. cm. -- (Government in action!)
    Includes bibliographical references and index.
    ISBN 1-59197-645-6
    1. Constitutional history--United States--Juvenile literature. 2. Constitutional law--United
States--Juvenile literature. [1. Constitutional history--United States. 2. Constitutional law--
United States. 3. United States. Constitution.] I. Title. II. Government in action! (ABDO
Publishing Company).

KF4541.Z9H36 2004
342.7302'9--dc22

                                                                                2003069309

Contents

The Constitution

The story of the Constitution began more than 200 years ago. The American colonists were fighting the Revolutionary War against England. They fought for freedom and a better way of life.

Once free from England, the colonists needed a central government. They first wrote a document called the Articles of **Confederation**. But it created a weak government. For this reason, the colonial leaders came together again. They wrote the United States Constitution.

The Constitution was designed to make all the states work together. It explains how one central, or federal, government unites them. And, it contains the country's basic laws.

The Constitution defines the United States we know today. It guides the American people in running their country. It also protects their rights and freedoms. The Constitution created a strong nation out of the 13 original colonies.

Opposite page: *A copy of the original Constitution*

We the People

of the United States, in order to form a more perfect Union, establish Justice, insure domestic Tranquility, provide for the common defence, promote the general Welfare, and secure the Blessings of Liberty to ourselves and our Posterity, do ordain and establish this Constitution for the United States of America.

Article I

Article II

Article III

Article IV

Article V

Article VI

Article VII

Birth of a Nation

The United States started in the 1600s as a group of British colonies. The colonies developed their own society, and England did not often interfere. But after the **French and Indian War**, England decided to tighten its control over the 13 colonies. It began by issuing new laws, as well as taxes, to help pay for the war.

In 1765, two new laws caused resentment in the colonies. The Quartering Act forced colonists to feed and house British soldiers. The Stamp Act required colonists to buy stamps for legal documents. But the people felt England could not tax them because the colonies did not have representatives in **Parliament**.

The Stamp Act was **repealed** the next year. But more taxes followed. The colonists began to fight back. They started **boycotting** British goods, and they started **riots**. In 1770, British soldiers fired into a crowd of colonists in the **Boston Massacre**.

England issued stamps similar to this one for the Stamp Act.

Colonists dressed as Native Americans throw tea into the harbor during the Boston Tea Party.

More taxes, including one on tea, continued to anger the colonists. On December 16, 1773, colonists dumped hundreds of chests of British tea into Boston Harbor. This became known as the Boston Tea Party.

After the Boston Tea Party, the English passed laws the colonists called the Intolerable Acts. The acts shut down Boston Harbor and reintroduced the Quartering Act. The colonists feared their freedoms were being taken away.

In September 1774, the First Continental Congress met in Philadelphia, Pennsylvania. Leaders from 12 of the 13 colonies gathered to discuss the troubles with England. They requested that England's king George III listen to their complaints.

But the king would not renew the colonists' freedoms. The situation with England grew worse. On April 19, 1775, colonists fought British troops at the Battles of Lexington and Concord. The Revolutionary War had begun.

On May 10, 1775, colonial leaders once again met in Philadelphia. The Second Continental Congress began acting as the colonies' government. It chose George Washington to lead the American army.

The congress also wanted to declare the colonies' independence. John Adams, Benjamin Franklin, Roger Sherman, Robert Livingston, and Thomas Jefferson worked together to create the Declaration of Independence. On July 4, 1776, the congress approved it.

The declaration stated that the American colonies were now a separate country from England. It said that a government should only exist with the permission of the people. It should protect their rights. To create such a government, the Second Continental Congress created the Articles of **Confederation.**

Thomas Jefferson

Thomas Jefferson was a delegate from Virginia to the Second Continental Congress. He was the main author of the Declaration of Independence. He wrote, "We hold these truths to be self-evident, that all men are created equal, that they are endowed by their Creator with certain unalienable Rights, that among these are Life, Liberty and the pursuit of Happiness." Jefferson later became U.S. secretary of state and president. He is also known for negotiating the Louisiana Purchase, and for sending Lewis and Clark on their journey.

Thomas Jefferson's face (second from left) is carved into Mount Rushmore in South Dakota. To the left of him is George Washington. To the right of Jefferson are Theodore Roosevelt and Abraham Lincoln.

The Confederation

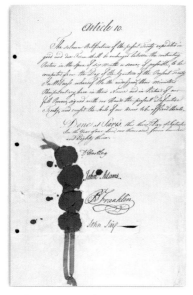

The Treaty of Paris ended the Revolutionary War in 1783.

The Revolutionary War continued for several more years. On October 19, 1781, the British army surrendered at the Battle of Yorktown. The war didn't officially end until 1783. But the English were defeated. America had earned its independence.

The colonies became 13 independent states. They were united by the Articles of **Confederation**. The last state had **ratified** this document in 1781, making it official.

The Articles of Confederation spelled out the powers of the states and the central government. Many of the former colonists feared creating a powerful central government like that of England. So, the articles gave most government power to the states.

The central government was called the **Confederation** Congress. It was made up of leaders elected by the people in each state. Each state had one vote. The congress could set up a post office and create money. It could also create a military, declare war, and make treaties.

Colonists cheer as George Washington and the Continental Army return to New York after the war.

Unfortunately, this government had many weaknesses. The **Confederation** Congress couldn't collect taxes or control foreign trade. There was no national court system. Nine states had to agree before any law could be passed. And, the government did not have the power to enforce laws once they were passed.

These weaknesses led to problems. Many states ignored or canceled laws made by the Confederation Congress. Because it could not collect taxes, the central government could not pay its **debts** from the Revolutionary War.

Pages from the Articles of Confederation

Without a strong central government, it was difficult to get the states to cooperate. The states started taxing goods from their neighbors. They printed too much of their own paper money, which led to **inflation**. Political leaders soon realized that the central government needed more power.

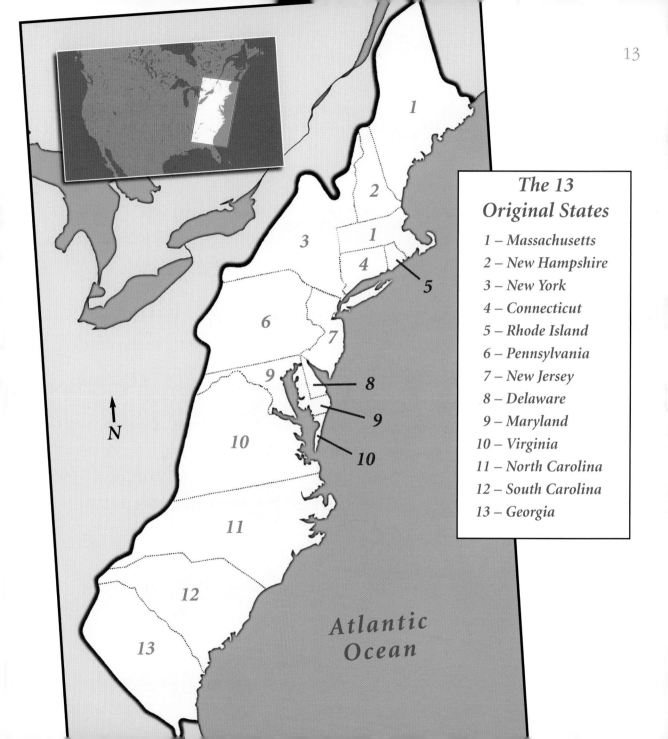

13

The 13 Original States

1 – Massachusetts
2 – New Hampshire
3 – New York
4 – Connecticut
5 – Rhode Island
6 – Pennsylvania
7 – New Jersey
8 – Delaware
9 – Maryland
10 – Virginia
11 – North Carolina
12 – South Carolina
13 – Georgia

N

Atlantic
Ocean

A New Government

In September 1786, a meeting was held in Annapolis, Maryland. Its purpose was to discuss amending the Articles of **Confederation**. However, delegates from only five states attended. Political leaders urged representatives from all the states to meet again in Philadelphia.

On May 25, 1787, leaders from almost every state met in the Pennsylvania State House for the Constitutional **Convention**. This time, only Rhode Island did not send delegates. The original plan was to fix the Articles of Confederation. Instead, they decided to make a whole new government.

To create this government, the framers of the Constitution first had to solve many issues. One of the biggest **debates** was over how strong the central government should be. Another difficult question was how the states would be represented. These issues were biggest between the large and the small states.

Opposite page: *The delegates met in this room during the Constitutional Convention of 1787.*

Large states such as New York and Virginia thought they should have the most say in the national government. This was because they had the most people. But, smaller states such as Delaware and New Hampshire were afraid that the bigger states would have too much power.

The Founding Fathers discuss a new government during the Constitutional Convention.

The Virginia Plan was an early idea for the Constitution. It said that each state would be represented in the legislature based on its population. So the more people that were in a state, the more representatives it would have. The small states refused to accept the plan.

Delegate William Paterson came up with the New Jersey Plan. This plan gave all the states an equal vote in the legislature. The big states didn't like the idea. They didn't believe the little states should have the same power as the big states.

The state delegates **debated** more plans and issues. Eventually, Roger Sherman and Oliver Ellsworth came up with the Connecticut Compromise. The idea was simple, but it satisfied both sides.

Under the compromise, the legislature would be split into two parts. The House of Representatives would represent states based on their population. The Senate would have an equal number of representatives from each state.

Even after the compromise, the framers had other difficult issues to solve. They debated slavery and how the president would be elected. Sometimes disagreements threatened to end the **convention**. But somehow, the group managed to find a balance of power between the states and the federal government.

Eventually the delegates compromised, and the document was written. Thirty-nine of the 55 elected delegates signed the United States Constitution on September 17, 1787. The next step was to convince the individual states to approve it.

The delegates' signatures at the end of the Constitution

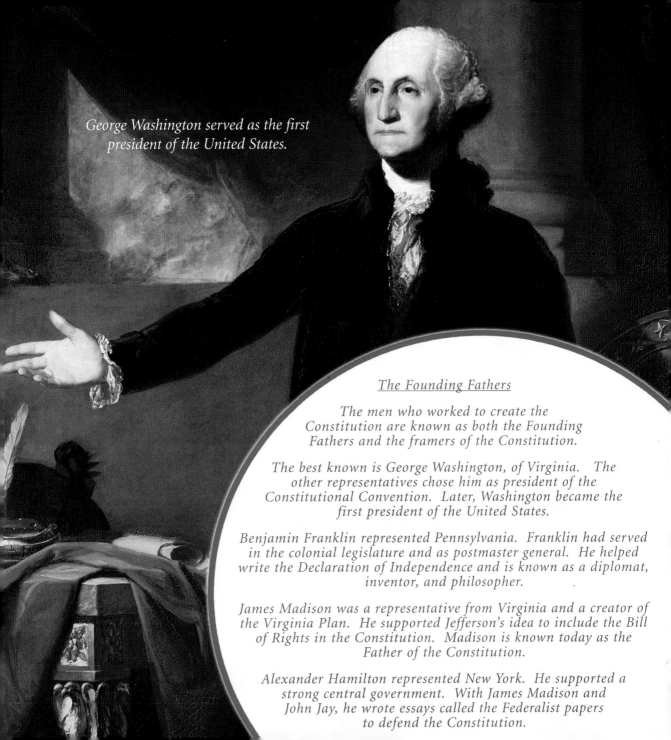

George Washington served as the first president of the United States.

<u>The Founding Fathers</u>

The men who worked to create the Constitution are known as both the Founding Fathers and the framers of the Constitution.

The best known is George Washington, of Virginia. The other representatives chose him as president of the Constitutional Convention. Later, Washington became the first president of the United States.

Benjamin Franklin represented Pennsylvania. Franklin had served in the colonial legislature and as postmaster general. He helped write the Declaration of Independence and is known as a diplomat, inventor, and philosopher.

James Madison was a representative from Virginia and a creator of the Virginia Plan. He supported Jefferson's idea to include the Bill of Rights in the Constitution. Madison is known today as the Father of the Constitution.

Alexander Hamilton represented New York. He supported a strong central government. With James Madison and John Jay, he wrote essays called the Federalist papers to defend the Constitution.

Ratification

Nine of the 13 states had to **ratify** the Constitution before it became law. **Debates** immediately sprang up between the Federalists, who were in favor of the Constitution, and the Anti-Federalists.

The opinions of both sides were printed in newspapers across the country. The most famous essays were the Federalist papers written by James Madison, Alexander Hamilton, and John Jay. New York newspapers printed the articles. They persuaded many people to support the Constitution.

A letter from George Washington to the government of Rhode Island, congratulating the state on its ratification of the Constitution

Some people thought the new national government would have too much power. They did not like that there wasn't a bill of rights to protect individual citizens. More people supported **ratification** once the Federalists agreed to add a bill of rights.

On June 21, 1788, the ninth state ratified the Constitution, making it official. Within two months, the important states of New York and Virginia had approved it as well. On May 29, 1790, Rhode Island became the last state to ratify. There were now 13 states in the United States of America.

Date Each State Ratified the Constitution

Delaware – *December 7, 1787*
Pennsylvania – *December 12, 1787*
New Jersey – *December 19, 1787*
Georgia – *January 2, 1788*
Connecticut – *January 9, 1788*
Massachusetts – *February 6, 1788*
Maryland – *April 28, 1788*
South Carolina – *May 23, 1788*
New Hampshire – *June 21, 1788*
Virginia – *June 25, 1788*
New York – *July 26, 1788*
North Carolina – *November 21, 1789*
Rhode Island – *May 29, 1790*

The Document

The Preamble

"We the People of the United States, in Order to form a more perfect Union, establish Justice, insure domestic Tranquility, provide for the common defense, promote the general Welfare, and secure the Blessings of Liberty to ourselves and our Posterity, do ordain and establish this Constitution for the United States of America."

The United States Constitution begins with the Preamble. This one sentence tells the purpose of the Constitution. It is followed by seven parts called articles. The articles define the different parts of the government and how they function.

The first three words of the Preamble remind Americans that their government is "by the people."

The articles state that the powers of the central government are separated into three branches. The first is the legislative branch. This is called Congress. The second is the executive branch, which is headed by the president. The third branch is the judicial branch. It is represented by the Supreme Court.

This separation of powers creates a system of checks and balances. It prevents one part of the government from getting too powerful. Each branch has power over the other two.

The Constitution also discusses the balance of power between the federal and state governments. It says that the federal government must protect the states. When laws conflict, the federal law is followed.

The Constitution created the presidency. The president leads the executive branch from the Oval Office inside the White House.

The Constitution is the law of the land. But it can be changed. The document itself allows future generations to modify the Constitution when needed.

ARTICLES OF THE CONSTITUTION

Article I states that Congress is the legislative body and is made up of the House of Representatives and the Senate. It explains how Congress is elected, what its powers are, and its power over the states.

Article II states that the president is the head of the executive branch. It tells who can be president and how the position is elected. It explains what the position's powers are and how the president can be removed from office.

Article III states that the Supreme Court is the country's judicial branch. It defines the Court's powers and jurisdiction. Article III also gives Congress the power to create lower federal courts.

Article IV protects citizens from unwarranted search and seizure. It guarantees citizens the same rights in all states. It says that the federal government will protect the states when needed. It also explains how new states can be added to the country.

Article V explains how the Constitution can be changed to meet future needs.

Article VI states that the Constitution is the supreme law of the land. If a state law conflicts with a federal law, the federal law is followed. This is true only if the law follows the Constitution.

Article VII explains the steps needed to ratify the Constitution.

Amendments

The Constitution wasn't perfect when it was created. For this reason, the Founding Fathers wisely added the ability to change it. These changes are called amendments.

An amendment must be approved by two-thirds of both houses of Congress. Next, the amendment must be approved by three-fourths of the states before it becomes law. Many amendments have been proposed over the years. But, only 27 of them have been **ratified**.

The first ten of these amendments went into effect in 1791. Together, they are called the Bill of Rights. The bill protects individuals from unfair actions of the government. Just a few of an American's rights are freedom of speech, the press, and religion.

Some amendments changed the way the U.S. government works. For example, the Seventeenth Amendment stated that a state's people could elect its senators, instead of the state legislature electing them. And, the Twenty-second Amendment limits a president to two terms in office.

The First Amendment allows the press the freedom to report any news, good or bad.

Constitutional amendments have also increased the freedoms of U.S. citizens. The Thirteenth Amendment ended slavery. The Nineteenth Amendment gave women the right to vote. These and other amendments have allowed the Constitution to keep up with changing times.

The Test of Time

The United States Constitution is the work of many dedicated people. These people had a goal they knew was important. The document they created is an excellent example of cooperation and compromise.

The Constitution the Founding Fathers wrote has lasted for more than 200 years. This is partly because of the amendment process. It makes the document flexible. This allows the Constitution to change with the will of the people it governs.

Another reason the Constitution has lasted is that the American people support it. They vote and perform their other **civic** duties. If the people did not exercise their rights, the government created by the Constitution would not function.

The United States government has stood the test of time. The Constitution has proven that a system of self-rule can work.

Opposite page: *The original Constitution is on guarded display in Washington, D.C.*

Glossary

Boston Massacre - March 5, 1770. English soldiers fired into a crowd of Boston colonists and killed five people.

boycott - to refuse to deal with a person, store, or organization until they agree to certain conditions.

civic - relating to citizenship.

Confederation - a group united for support or common action.

convention - a large meeting set up for a special purpose.

debate - to discuss a question or topic, often publicly.

debt - something owed to someone, usually money.

French and Indian War - from 1754 to 1763. A series of battles fought for control of land in North America. England and its colonies fought against France, its colonies, and several Native American tribes.

inflation - a rise in the price of goods and services.

Parliament - England's highest lawmaking body.

ratify - to officially approve.

repeal - to formally withdraw or cancel.

riot - a sometimes violent disturbance caused by a large group of people.

Web Sites

To learn more about the United States Constitution, visit ABDO Publishing Company on the World Wide Web at **www.abdopub.com**. Web sites about the Constitution are featured on our Book Links page. These links are routinely monitored and updated to provide the most current information available.

Paul Revere rides to warn the colonists of the British invasion, beginning the fight for independence that led to the making of the Constitution.

Index